The Art of Pastoring

Contemplative Reflections

The Art of Pastoring

Contemplative Reflections

William C. Martin

Book design by David Skinner, indelible inc.

Published by CTS Press, P.O. Box 520, Decatur, GA 30031

Printed in the United States of America

Dedicated to my wife, Nancy,
a United Methodist pastor
who comes closer to living
the truths of this book
than anyone else I know.

FOREWORD

In considering the various influences that led me to this volume I must first acknowledge my heritage and training, which instilled in me a deep love for the Word of God— both the written Word and the Incarnate Word. My seminary training embraced the Reformed tradition, through which I was exposed to many mentors, teachers and authors who formed in me an awareness of the Bible's power to communicate the grace of God.

It is this grace of God that sometimes becomes forgotten in the crunch of pastoral responsibilities. The Bible can become a tool for grinding out yet another lesson or another sermon, usually without our taking enough time to truly appreciate what we read or hear. The Living Word must move within to refresh the heart of the pastor, even as the flowing stream refreshes the land, so the written words of Scripture may once again come to life. My work as a retreat master and spiritual director has led me on a search for ways to facilitate this refreshment. I have discovered that the Living Word sometimes finds unusual vehicles.

Such a vehicle for me has been the semi-legendary Sixth Century B.C. Chinese sage, Lao Tzu. The wisdom of his classic, *Tao Te Ching*, is pre-Christian and does not present a theology as such. But I have lived with it for several years now and I can testify that it is filled with the grace of the Creator and its gentle advice flows from the Sophia, the Wisdom that danced with God in the beginning.

Unlike Western management texts. *Tao Te Ching* uses few words and makes no attempt to explain or give a rationale for its premises. The wisdom is given in short, figurative, sometimes vague or even paradoxical statements. In writing my own rendition of Lao Tzu's wisdom I have attempted to be faithful to this style.

Jesus taught in this same tradition. He presented the wondrous truths of the Gospel in images, parables, and paradoxes. He did not attempt to satisfy linear logic. His words danced and pirouetted and refused to be pinned down—not because he wanted to be deliberately evasive, but because the Truth he proclaimed was of Dimensions beyond our space and of Eternity beyond our time.

I have taken the traditional 81 chapters of Lao Tzu's original work, absorbed the message of each, and attempted to translate the essence of each thought into a message for the Western pastor. The words, style, and applications in the book are mine. The wisdom is that of Lao Tzu. I am grateful to the Spirit of God, working through him, for supplying such graceful ideas. I hope I have passed them on with reasonable faithfulness.

I am also grateful for two excellent translations of *Tao Te Ching*: one by Witter Bynner and the other by Stephen Mitchell. These works have been my constant companions for several years.

Many colleagues and friends have read this manuscript and offered excellent suggestions. I am in their debt as well.

My final debt is to the countless thousands of men and women clergy who labor in the most difficult of all professions. It is my love for the many clergy whose lives have touched mine, and my compassion for the others whose stories I will never know, that has fueled this book.

Bill Martin
Phoenix, Arizona

TO THE PASTOR

"Being a pastor is like being a stray dog at a whistler's convention."

- Anonymous

This is how it is!

Everyone who has served or is serving as a clergyperson in the Western world knows this feeling— knows how impossible the task seems at times.

There was a time when it promised to be rewarding and fulfilling. People would hang on your every word. They would appreciate the sacrifices you would make, and you would therefore make them gladly. Church growth would occur automatically because people would be filled with gratitude for the inspiration, comfort, and truth you would give them.

Instead the job has become thankless and impossible at times. In the midst of it even your own spirituality has become a victim. I know. I have been there. And I have also heard the stories of countless other clergy during my years of practice as a counselor and spiritual director. We have all struggled.

By calling attention to the wisdom of the *Tao Te Ching,* I am not advocating an abandonment of the essential truths of Christianity for some Eastern or "New Age" doctrinal hodgepodge. Jesus was far more Eastern in his teachings than we often realize, and if we can recover this aspect of our Christian heritage, we may be able to correct some of the stresses caused by an overly Western approach to the pastorate. Perhaps our Western approach has erred on the "Martha" side of our profession and we may need to cultivate some of Mary's quietness and openness before our Lord.

I know this: You don't need another success manual that will bring you ten more tidy tips on how to "do it right this time." I would be guilty of cruelty and fraud if I foisted another layer of "should" upon your already burdened soul.

Although I have endeavored to make my reflections on the pre-Christian material of Lao Tzu faithful to Biblical truth, I have not included Scripture references for each individual chapter. As you read these meditations I trust that you will sense the Biblical wisdom flowing throughout.

I have tried to point you in the direction from which I received the help that enabled me to rediscover my soul. (It was there all the time.) Understand, I am merely pointing. I cannot tell you how to regain your soul within your ministry. I can only point.

Thought 1 - The Word

> You are a minister of the Word
> but not of words.
> The Word was in the beginning before words
> and beyond words.
> And whether they weave sophisticated patterns
> of intellectual magic,
> or they strike with passion
> at the heart of the people's emotions,
> words are not Word
> For the Word is inexhaustible.
> One can only stand in wonder
> and point.

Observations

I have used "Word" to communicate an essential element of Lao Tzu's thought. The Chinese is best translated as "way," but the concept is an important bridge to the Christian truth of the eternal Logos, the creative power of God. As I use the term in the following chapters I refer to the Christian understanding of "Word" as the Logos of God so beautifully praised in the first chapter of John.

Because our profession so depends on the use of language to persuade and entertain, we easily fall into the illusion that we have defined the Eternal Word with our words and concepts. Jesus incarnates the Word but does not exhaust the Word. The Word still dances in the cosmos; is still creating stars and galaxies; is still guiding the universe toward its destiny; and is still beyond our ability to describe.

Thought 2 - Priorities

To consider your preaching
of more importance than the opening of a flower
is to leave the narrow path.
To value certain appointments on your daily calendar
and resent others as intrusions
is to misunderstand the Word.
To esteem and enjoy some people in your parish
and to discount and dismiss others
is to wobble blindly.
To meet the needs of others
and ignore the whispers of your own soul
is to succumb to the illusion
that there is a time more precious than now,
and a place more heavenly
than here.

Observations
There are two questions that need to be answered in order to move along the path toward God. One could spend a lifetime just considering these two questions and answers.

> The first question is, "What time is it?"
> The second question is, "Where are you?"
> The **only** correct answer to the first is, "**Now!**"
> The **only** correct answer to the second is, "**Here!**"

Thought 3 - Visions

A wise pastor does not inspire the people
with grand visions
for the visions will become idols.
A prudent minister will not call attention to achievement
for that will separate people into "achievers"
and "non-achievers."
The follower of the Word will not encourage
displays of wealth
for all will be dissatisfied.
But the one who serves the Word
will quiet the noisy heart,
clarify sight,
simplify the busy life,
and reduce the plethora of needs
so the people may see clearly and with purity
without being pushed or pulled.
The parish becomes holy on its own.

Observations
The congregation does not need great visions or dreams. Of much more value is the pastor who calls attention to the gentle breeze caressing the flowers by the front door; who calms the troubled waters of grief and fear; who speaks a word that heals. You are not called to bring inspiration to people. Rather loosen the tightness in their chest that restricts their breathing, and their lungs will gratefully expand of their own accord and they will inspire themselves.

Thought 4 - Mystery

Do not forget that you serve
a Mystery
that neither you nor your father's father
nor your mother's mother began.
And the laughter and the tears
that accompany your labor
are not born
of your cleverness
or your holiness,
but are reflections of the Mystery of God
in the still waters
of the eternal lake
by moonlight.
The God you serve is like an eternal lake
whose waters are always calm and clear like glass,
reflecting truth to all who gaze upon them.
A million million reflections
and the lake remains the same.
It is not your job to stir the waters
but to show the way to the lakeside.

Observations

Remember the Mystery. Never forget the Mystery. Your rational education is a great gift, but it will never reveal the depths of the Spirit to you or to anyone else. If you continue to stir the waters with this new program or that great project, the people will never be able to see the reflection.

Thought 5 - Judgment

The Divine Word dances in the spaces
between all the atoms of the Universe
and binds together all that is
and fills the lungs of saint and sinner alike.
The wise pastor inhales the Holy Spirit,
and releases all judgment with each breath.
Therefore it is not helpful for a pastor
to chatter on about this person or that person.
He does not show his ignorance
with endless commentary
but lets God speak
in his own silence.

Observations
I have noticed that, in attempting to avoid taking sides, many pastors
end up trying to please both sides. This is like standing with one foot
in one drifting rowboat and one foot in another drifting rowboat. The
boats will go their own way regardless and the pastor will end up in
the water. Better to stand on the dock and stay out of either boat.

Thought 6 - Birthing

The Word is the eternal Feminine,
the source of all life
giving birth to new wonders
within all people
at all times.
And the pastor is the midwife
who brings comfort and encouragement
to all who are in labor.

Observations

You are not a pastor so that you might give birth to your own dreams for the church. The birth pangs of the people in your parish must be your primary concern. It is helpful when talking with any member of your congregation to reflect within yourself, "To what is this person giving birth?"

Thought 7 - Acceptance

Before the beginning was the Word.
After the ending will be the Word.
Beyond all beginning and ending is the Word.
Without desire for itself is the Word,
so the Word has no need of a particular response
from any particular person.
People may be exactly as they are
in the presence of the Word
without fear of judgment.

The pastor has no need to impress
and so is free to be with her people;
has no need to be out front
and so is with the people;
has nothing to lose,
and so is at perfect peace.

Observations

The Chair of your Board of Trustees thinks you are incompetent. The Tuesday morning Bible study wishes you would attend more often. The chair of the Pulpit Committee has suggested that you "might want to pep up your sermons a little, if you know what I mean."

Do you need to change to make these people happy? No! Might you consider change within your own heart? Yes.

Do they need to change to make your life more serene? No! Might you find serenity within your own heart? Yes.

Thought 8 - Water-Way

The perfect pastor is like water
bringing nourishment to all he touches
without effort or trying.
Like water, he seeks out the lowest places
while the foolish pastor strives and strains
to climb the highest places.

Live modestly.
Keep your thinking serene and simple.
Bestow grace upon yourself and others.
Never try to control your congregation.
In your vocation, do that which you most enjoy
for it will be your best gift to others.
And when you are with those you love,
let your soul and mind be where your body is.

Observations

Water's power lies in its ability to be fully what it is, where it is. It may be obstructed but never distracted.

Make a list of the distractions that are currently part of your life. Where does your mind wander? How often? Why? Distractions usually come to the pastor because he believes that life must be complicated in order to be productive. Nonsense!

If you are never where you are, you will have no power. If you cultivate the ability to be where you are, you will move mountains to the sea as patiently and as surely as does your sister water.

Thought 9 - Rest

If you fill your calendar with important appointments
you will have no time for God.
If you fill your spare time with essential reading
you will starve your soul.
If you fill your mind with worry
about budgets and offerings,
the pains in your chest and the ache in your shoulders
will betray you.
If you try to conform to the expectations
of those around you
you will be forever their slave.
Work a modest day
then step back and rest.
This will keep you close to God.

Observations

One of the first things I look at when I begin spiritual direction with a pastor is his or her daily planner. It reveals volumes about that pastor's spiritual condition, values, fears, and ambitions. It tells me who their bosses are, who their lover is, and how much value they place on their soul. If you're working more than 50 hours a week, you're not doing it for God no matter how eloquent your rationalizations.

Take a long, prayerful, meditative look at your calendar. Who are you trying to impress? God? Give me a break. The congregation? Possibly. Yourself? Bingo!

Now cut some big chunks out of each week for family, rest, meditation, prayer, and flower sniffing. When you've done that we'll talk more about the path to God.

Thought 10 - Abilities

A minister of the Word has certain abilities:
the ability to gently return a noisy mind
to a quiet place of communion with God;
the ability to release tension from the body
and to remain supple and relaxed;
the ability to cleanse the soul
of accumulated negativity
so the pure light of God is undimmed;
the ability to lead the people in the parish
without needing them to behave as you see fit;
the ability to let even the most important events unfold
without worrying or tampering with the process;
the ability to detach from your own plans for the church
and see the grace of God unfold
in a gentle way.
And if you are truly among the wisest of pastors
you create a safe place for your people's creativity;
you guide without agenda;
and you enjoy all without possessing any.

Observations
These are not the kind of abilities that come naturally in the parish.
They are seldom found on a pastoral search committee's list of hiring
criteria. You will have to develop a deep conviction that they are of
value and stick to them when everyone is clamoring for a piece of your
flesh. God bless you.

Thought 11 - Emptying

It is the invisible center
where the spokes of the wheel meet
that allows the wheel to move.
The pastor becomes invisible
so that the parish may move freely.

It is the empty space within
that makes the bowl useful.
The pastor empties herself of agenda and expectation
so that the Spirit of God may fill her.

It is the space within the walls of a house
that gives a family room to live.
The pastor creates a space,
uncluttered by "oughts" or "shoulds"
where her people may safely live.

It is the invisible, empty, spacious pastor
who serves the Word.
Don't be misled by much ado.

Observations
Emptying is difficult for the Western pastor. It is likely that you have become convinced that your worth lies in the fullness of your mind, your schedule, and your congregation's programs. Yet if you do not become empty you will never be whole.

What can you pour out? How can you begin to empty yourself?

Thought 12 - Striving

Seeking to look attractive creates blindness.

Seeking to sound impressive creates deafness.

Seeking to please all creates tastelessness.

Seeking to control creates thoughtlessness.

Seeking to protect dreams creates heartlessness.

The pastor sees the events within the parish

and hears the voice of the people,

but trusts only her inner wisdom

and acts only from her own soul.

Externals drift in and out of her open,

welcoming, non-possessive heart.

Observations

May I again call attention to the calendar as a window on the soul? Do a searching, fearless, and honest analysis of your activities of the past week – every single one.

Which of them, in the secret honesty of your heart, have been largely concerned with image, people-pleasing, control, and security? Which have truly emerged from your own soul's treasure?

Thought 13 - Climbing

Do not seek to climb the ladder
of ecclesiastical success.
Ladders are always shaky
and lead down as well as up.
Keep your feet on the ground.
Only then will you hear the Word
and not lose your balance.

Beware of inspiring either hope
or fear in your congregation.
Hope can be the projection of our own desires
which is idolatry.
Fear will immobilize people
and block the flow of love.
Understand that there is nothing to strive for,
hope for,
or fear.
For all is as it should be, right here, right now,
for here and now is the house of the Spirit of God.

Observations

I know that there are many things you want to change, to fix, to make right. There are goals you want to reach, dreams you want to realize. But be careful. Such things have their place but first make sure you can answer this question,

"How is it, **now**, with your soul?"

with a firm, "It is well with my soul!"

Thought 14 - Impossible Task

If you try to show it to your congregation,
no one will see it.
If you try to preach it to your congregation,
no one will hear it.
If you try to lead your congregation to it,
it will slip through everyone's fingers.

How does one describe that which cannot be contained?
How does one approach that which has no beginning?
How can one lose that which is without end?
Relax and return to your soul
for it has always known its home,
and you will give your people your gift of Wisdom.

Observations
Your task is impossible. Consider the demands:

> "Show us God."
> "Tell us what God wants."
> "Lead us to God."

If you think you can do these things you are already deceived. But you *can* find your own soul and perhaps show others how to do that. To their surprise they will satisfy their demands on their own.

Thought 15 - Qualities

The qualities of a pastor are impossible to describe.
We can only see them in action.
No noise or clamor, but a careful manner of moving
through the daily parish activities;
clear eyes steadily seeing to the heart;
kindness and humility in the presence of others,
needing to defend nothing, prove nothing –
therefore able to respond
with the sureness of the flowing river.
Hiding nothing,
therefore able to speak truthfully with ease.
Can you do this?
Can you wait patiently
until all the voices that clamor for action settle down?
Can you resist the temptation
to do what the parish seems so desperately
to want you to do
until the Spirit of God reveals
naturally and gently the next step,
and events unfold as they should,
without pushing or shoving?
The pastor does not seek success.
She does not see people as tokens to be collected.
Since she does not seek these things,
she is available at the level of the soul to all who seek.

Thought 16 - Home

Watch the events within the parish
with detachment and serenity.
For all events are of a common origin
and share a common destination.
The smallest thought and greatest dream
return to their home in God.
To live at home is to know true peace.
Your people are longing for home.
But they wander in confusion and sorrow.
If you are living at home you create for them
a space where they may find:
tolerance, dignity, kindness, acceptance,
all the qualities of a home governed by love.
If you remain at home,
nothing can displace you or bother you,
and when you die, even then you will be unperturbed
for you will still be at home.

Observations
The Western mind insists on the separation of heaven and earth. Jesus
has reconciled all things. You cannot create a heaven on earth, but you
can *recognize* heaven in earth. Your task is to unmask earth to reveal
heaven; to unmask the most difficult person in your church to reveal
God.

Thought 17 - Congregation

When your congregation despises you,

it is a great sorrow.

When your congregation holds you in awe,

it seems somewhat better.

When your congregation praises you far and wide,

it seems even better still.

But when your congregation hardly notices

that you exist,

you have become a pastor.

How do you feel about your congregation

deep within your heart?

That is what they will become.

When the pastor's work is done,

the congregation will truthfully say,

"We did it ourselves."

And the pastor will rejoice.

Observations

You are not a performer. Yet much of your job structure sets you up for evaluation as a performer. Can you change any of this? One thing that has helped many pastors is to greet people before rather than after the service, eliminating the "receiving line" atmosphere. What other things keep you needlessly in the limelight?

Thought 18 - Opposites

If your congregation does not know the Word
they will be greatly concerned with right and wrong.
If they do not experience grace,
they will argue constantly about proper doctrine.
If they do not live in harmony with one another,
they will talk endlessly about love.
If their life as a congregation is dying,
they will concern themselves with church growth.

Observations
You can be reasonably sure that whatever a congregation's pet subject is, they are experiencing its opposite deep within their souls. A healthy congregation seldom talks about growth, morality, or doctrine – they are too busy living the Truth behind the words.

Thought 19 - Pressure

Do you think you make your people holy and healthy
by constantly preaching about their need to change?
Do you increase the peace of God within the church
by constant pressure to do more, give more, be more?
Eliminate the pressure to change
and people will mature according to their own soul.
Eliminate the pressure to give
and people will give from their own hearts
to the needs of other hearts.
Eliminate the pressure to grow and achieve
and people will become wise, spiritual and content.
Above all else, stay close to the Heart of God
and all things around you will unfold as they should.

Observations

A pastor I know had the courage to replace the annual "every member financial pledge" drive with a simple response sheet that asked each person to reflect deeply on ways they would "seek the Kingdom of God" in the coming year. Finances were not mentioned. Giving increased 15 percent.

Thought 20 - Face Yourself

Why so much concern
about the problems of the church?
Why have you slipped into this trap?
Why are you so anxious for success,
so terrified of failure?
Have not these terms been rendered meaningless
by our Lord?
People get excited about the latest book,
by the great youth program down at Central Church,
by the new sanctuary at First Church.
You alone remain calm and detached,
neither envious nor pleased.
People create distractions and playthings.
You face the inner emptiness for them.
You are a fool for their sake.
People devise clever financial schemes
and build great monuments to greed and ego.
You have set aside ego to search for soul
and seem dull and dark to them.
You achieve nothing they deem worthy.
You seem to them to drift,
blown at the mercy of the wind.
You cannot live the same as others,
for your food, and strength, and life
come from your Lord and God.

Thought 21 - Shining Through

A true pastor shines with peace and love,
because he is always in communion with the Word.

He is at one with the Word
because he does not depend on words.
The Word Itself shines through him.

Since words do not exhaust the Word
and the Word is more than mere ideas,
how does he know even these words are true?
Because he looks inside himself.

Observations
Are there ways in which you can lessen your dependence upon words? Can you cut your sermon time by ten percent? Can you include longer periods of silence in your pastoral prayers? Can you listen more at the pot luck rather than succumbing to the feeling that you must be *on* all the time? Can you just sit with someone in the hospital rather than fill the air with comforting words?

Thought 22 - Paradoxes

If you want to bring healing to your people,
show that you are wounded.
If you want them to do what is right,
show that you have done wrong.
If you want them to be filled with God,
show that you are empty.
If you want them to have life abundant,
show them how to die.
If you want everything good for them,
show them how to give everything up.

When Jesus said, "You must die in order to live,"
he spoke a basic truth.
There is no other road to life.

Observations
Jesus was a master of the use of paradox. In this he was solidly in the Eastern tradition of non-linear apprehension of knowledge. Don't try to "figure out" paradoxes. Live with them and let their seeming non-rationality quiet down the overactive synapses of your beleaguered left brain. The pastorate is a paradox itself; a non-linear vocation in the midst of a linear world.

Thought 23 - At One With

Whatever you do as a pastor, do fully.
If you express yourself in words,
do it completely
then be quiet.
There is no need for continued pushing and shoving.

If you let yourself be at one with the Word,
you will be at one with all things,
and you will do all things completely and naturally.
You will be at one with your strengths
and use them appropriately and completely
without fanfare or need for approval.
You will be at one with your weaknesses
and live them completely
without need for avoidance or complaint.
You will be at one with your gains and your losses,
living each completely, accepting both,
seeing all things with tranquility.

When you cry, you will cry.
When you laugh, you will laugh.
When you are angry, you will be angry.
When you dance, you will dance.
You will be who you are, where you are
and your people will know that all things will be well.

Thought 24 - Work

If you stretch yourself out and reach for the stars
as all the success manuals would have you do,
you will be continuously off-balance
and your congregation will wobble to and fro,
never knowing peace.
If you push them to achieve,
no one will advance far along the path of maturity.
If you continually call attention
to your long hard hours of work on their behalf,
your reputation will diminish.
If you are always confident of success,
you are in denial.
If you have a position of great power
and respect within the church,
you have no power within yourself.
If you see your work as more important
and godly than anything else,
you are building your life on quicksand.

If you want to be a wise and true minister of the Word,
work a modest number of hours each week,
then go home.

Observations
There will be a hundred voices saying, "There is more yet to do," to every one that says, "Go home."   Listen carefully.

Thought 25 - Security

God is the birther of the universe.
Before the universe was born,
the solitary, infinite, changeless, formless, eternal
God
was!
And this creator of all
flows inside your church,
outside your church,
through your church,
and binds your church to the beginning of all things.
So your pastorate,
your congregation,
and your life
are all bound to the beginning and to the end.
Why then would you ever think that
your position, or your congregation, or your life
needed protection?
For God flows through the universe,
into your church,
into you,
and back to God.
No beginning, no end.

Thought 26 - Movement

If you wish to create movement

within the lives of your people,

you must remain unmoved,

a source of tranquility and a place of rest.

Is it really important that you serve

on one more committee or denominational board?

You are creating for yourself the illusion of movement

and the pretense of importance.

There is no need for pretense.

Your importance is real and dwells within you.

Your gift to your people is who you are.

Let your restlessness pass

until the waters of the eternal lake

are calm once again.

Observations
Can you sit still, completely still, for five minutes - no movement of any sort? No adjustment of position, no tension anywhere - just peaceful sitting or kneeling; arms relaxed, head resting comfortably on top of the spine, nothing moving except quiet breathing - yet nothing tense or rigid. If you can do this twice each day you will begin to create room for the Spirit of God to speak.

Thought 27 - Openness

The pastor embodies the Light.
He is open to all situations
and spends no time wishing things were different.
He receives all people
and spends no time wishing they were different.
For the Light sees no good or bad people,
only loved or unloved people.
The pastor who makes distinctions
will get lost amidst his judgments.

Observations
If you must make distinctions within your parish, try this exercise. On a sheet of paper make two columns. Label the left column, *Enough Love* and the right, *Shortage of Love*. Go through your membership list and place people in one category or the other as honestly as you can based on whether or not you think they receive enough love in their lives. You now have people categorized in the only manner that is ever helpful. Keep this list before you and make the right hand column a matter of prayer.

Thought 28 - Better Things

It is good to know your strength and power,
but always return to dwell in your flexibility.
For if you hold the church in your arms
as a mother cradles a child,
the Spirit of God will flow freely through you.

It is good to have achievement,
but always return to anonymity.
For you are a model for those in your parish
and they cannot see the Word
if your own light is blinding.

It is good to have friends within the church,
but always return to solitude.
For in your solitude you see the world as it is
and you accept its pain
and feel its wounds.

Observations
For flexibility: Dance or exercise in a slow, flowing, meditative manner.
For anonymity: Take your name off the church sign and stop presiding at every meeting.
For solitude: There are no short cuts. You must be alone, truly alone, for extended periods of time on a regular basis.

Thought 29 - Change

Do not seek to improve people.
It cannot be done.
To seek to improve someone
is to treat them as an object.
If you treat people as objects,
you will lose them.

The Scriptures say,
"There is a time for every purpose under heaven."
Let the time for everything come and go.
People will be sad, and happy;
full of vigor, and exhausted;
peaceful, and anxious;
rich, and poor.
Let all these things come and go
without trying to control them.
Stay at the center of the Word
and your people will have a place
to safely be themselves.

Observations
Your soul may compel you to change and grow.
Another's soul may compel him to change and grow.
But you cannot, must not, compel another's soul.
Believe me even when all evidence seems to point to the contrary, your people are perfect, *just as they are.* The Holy Spirit will bring whatever change and growth is necessary.

Thought 30 - Conflict

By its very nature
the parish will contain conflict.
Not everyone will appreciate or value
the work of the wise pastor.
Some will choose to see him as the enemy:
someone to be challenged, criticized,
and defeated.
Do not subscribe to the illusion inherent
in such conflict.
If you try to impose your will by the force
of your winning personality,
or clever arguments,
or worse, the righteousness of your cause,
you will reap the whirlwind.
Give the gift that is yours to give,
then withdraw from the conflict.
Your parish will always be beyond
your ability to control.
The opinion of others will forever lie
outside of your capacity to change.
Because you love your own soul,
are content with your own soul,
and accept your own soul,
you have no need to defend or to defeat.
The parish returns to the Word and goes on.

Thought 31 - Attack

Will the time ever come
when you must defend yourself
within your congregation?
Will the slings and arrows
of frightened people ever cause you
to attack in return?
Perhaps,
but only out of greatest necessity,
and with immense restraint.
And never with rejoicing or satisfaction.
For when the smoke clears,
and the bodies are counted,
it will be a time for mourning.

Observations
I have often wished that martial arts were taught in seminary. They provide a physical discipline which, when coupled with Christian spiritual discipline, provides countless lessons in practical pastoral care. As a martial arts student, I was taught that a true artist strikes only under extreme necessity and always with the minimum force necessary to protect himself. I was also taught that if I ever have to strike, I have lost.

Thought 32 - Temporary

Your role as a pastor
and your congregation's life as a church
will both come to an end.
Only the Word is without end.
Therefore be aware of the temporary
and never give it too much importance.
If people gave less attention to the multitude of things
temporary,
and more attention to the One thing
permanent,
there would be room in their hearts
for the writing of the Word
and there would be no more need to teach
for all would know.

Observations
Whatever you are worried about right now, whatever is distracting you at this moment – it is temporary. Relax.

Thought 33 - Good or Wise?

You are told that the good pastor
will know her people well.
But the wise pastor knows herself well.

You are told that the good pastor
will inspire her people to goodness.
But the wise pastor inspires herself to truth.

You are told that the good pastor
will bring great accomplishments to her parish.
But the wise pastor already has accomplished all.

You are told that the good pastor
will bring new life to the congregation.
But the wise pastor teaches them how to die to live.

Observations
Your people are longing for wisdom. Are you planning to give them
another program instead?

Thought 34 - True Greatness

The parish that is filled with the Word

gives birth to countless wonderful things,

yet it lays no claim to them.

It brings nurture to many people,

yet it does not seek to count them.

Its work permeates the hearts of the community,

yet the community does not know it is there,

they only know that they feel content.

This parish and this pastor

do not know that they are great.

The community does not know

that they are great.

Therefore they are truly great.

Observations

How blessed are the countless thousands of little congregations who quietly go about the business of giving their modest gift to the world.

For the souls of those pastors whose congregations are large and powerful, we pray to the Lord. Lord have mercy.

Thought 35 - What People Say

The pastor who truly knows her soul

is in harmony with all that is –

pain and pleasure –

and therefore sees no need to call attention to herself.

She does not use words that inspire admiration.

Her people do not say,

"You must come hear our wonderful pastor,

she is so eloquent!"

She is so familiar with her own soul,

with the Voice of God within her life,

that her parishioners say,

"God loves me."

Observations

People want to praise and admire their pastor. Do not succumb to their desire. *You* want praise and admiration. Do not succumb to your desire.

Can you figure out a way to go through a whole week of parish work with as little attention called to yourself or to your position as possible? Use some creativity. How anonymous can you be?

Thought 36 - Fires

If there is discontent within your parish,
you must allow it room to breathe.
If you seek to repress or to ignore it,
it will smolder forever.
If you let it burn without fearing it,
it will blaze up
and die for lack of fuel.
Since you have nothing to fear,
and nothing to prove,
you can practice this difficult truth
and see how great the results will be.

Observations

A pastor with extreme anxiety came to me and reported that he spent most of his time, "putting out fires." Putting out fires is a common task in our profession, but it is not always the best thing to do.

Discontent is a wonderful gift. It tells us something. Let it burn openly. If it is deep and valid it will burn and cleanse the underbrush and prepare for new growth. If it is superficial and false, it will find no fuel and burn out quickly.

Thought 37 - Artificial Need

The natural Word is distorted
by artificial creation of need
on the part of users of words
on behalf of sellers of goods.

If you, the pastor, are not distorted
by attachment to the need to achieve,
your people will gradually settle
into natural patterns of peace.

Observations
Examine carefully your programs, your committees, your tasks.

"Is what we are about to do really necessary? Or is it just continuing to create the illusion of busyness and productivity?"

Holiness, Goodness, and Peace are not programmatic.

Thought 38 - Illusions

There are powerful illusions that hinder

the working of the Word through a pastor:

The illusion that there is something to achieve.

The illusion that there is something to lose.

The illusion that there is something to do.

If you believe there is something you must achieve

within the parish,

you will never achieve it.

If you believe you have something to lose,

you will lose it.

If you believe there is something that must be done

in order for God to be pleased with your life,

you will never get it done.

Instead lead your people

beside the still waters of their souls.

There they will find for themselves the Reality

behind the illusion

and they will be blessed.

Observations

Illusions are persistent creatures. We have taken a long time putting them in place and we will not let go of them easily. Achievement and productivity are among the most tenacious of these illusions. Failure and vacations are the best antidotes I know.

Thought 39 - Image

If the pastor is the polished gem
in the middle of the parish,
the people will be distracted
and blinded by his brightness.
Rather let him be as a common rock,
simple and plain.
And his people will see the wondrous sky,
the sparkling waters,
the verdant forests,
unspoiled by humanity's attempts to polish
and interfere with the natural flow of the Word.
This will restore their souls.

Observations
You don't have the time or energy available to keep shining your image. That is not your calling. Let your possessions, clothes, words, and manner be plain and natural.

Thought 40 - Peace

Stop fretting.
Be quiet.
Learn peace.
Birth peace.

Thought 41 - Foolishness

A true pastor hears the Word,
and begins to live its truths
for they already existed in her soul.

Another pastor hears the Word,
and finds it appealing but impractical
for she has learned differently.

Yet still another pastor hears the Word,
and dismisses it entirely as absurd nonsense,
for she is deeply lost.

You must lead your people into the dark,
in order for them to see the light.
You must take them back to their souls,
in order for them to go forward.
You must face criticism for being weak,
inconsistent, indifferent, and unsophisticated,
in order to show true power,
stability, love and wisdom.
Can you do this?

Observations

Paul was willing to be a "fool for Christ's sake." Your congregation will want you to appear wise, practical, and strong. There may be times when you must appear foolish, impractical, and weak. You will need to remain close to the Spirit of God to do this. Good luck.

Thought 42 - Solitude

Within the parish lie two energies,
the Active and the Passive.
And a place of solitude is needed
for these two to meet and conceive.

The pastor is not afraid of the place of solitude.
He seeks it out
and gives himself to it,
knowing it is the womb
from which the life of his church is born.

Observations

I know a pastor who spends three full days each month in desert solitude at a silent retreat center.

    No books.
    No tapes.
    No radio.
    No TV.
    Just a journal.

How long can you go without a book or some other form of external stimulus? The answer may contain a measure of your awareness of your soul.

Thought 43 - Doing/Being

How would you pastor
if you could not speak?
How would you love the parish
if you were immobilized in bed?
If you can answer these questions,
you know the truth of your calling.
If you can do these things,
you will overcome all obstacles.

Observations

These questions cannot be answered easily. They are like Zen koans in their seeming impossibilities. Jesus used koans often in his teaching, much to the dismay of the rationalists of his time who cared little about camels passing through eyes of needles.

Treat these words like koans and let them rest in the back of your mind for days, weeks, or months. Then, almost unbidden, insight and wisdom will spring up from the deeper recesses of the unconscious realm of the soul. You will begin to discern the difference between doing and be-ing.

Thought 44 - Just As I Am

Does your soul long to be well known
and greeted by colleagues with reverence and awe?
Does it hunger for material reward,
finding there reassurance and security?

Or does it accept the congregation,
and your situation,
and you,
just as they are?
What freedom in knowing
that there is nothing to gain!

Observations
"How will things ever change if I accept them as they are?"

Paradox again. Try it this week with the most frustrating situation within your congregation. Adopt the attitude that there is nothing that needs to change. Pay careful attention to what happens.

Thought 45 - Perfection

To be perfectly yourself while doing your work
is to do that work perfectly.
To notice fully what you are doing right now
is to be filled with God.

Don't be misled by what seems flawed
and ordinary in parish life.
Don't succumb to old definitions of perfection.
By being perfectly at ease with what is,
you will allow the Word to create
that which is not.

Observations
Stop beating up on yourself! I know you do. For all your belief in the
grace of God, you seldom apply it to yourself.

> *To become perfect you only need to cease*
> *striving for perfection.*

It is *God* who will bring his good work in you to completion.

45

Thought 46 - Fear

Fear is the great illusion
and destroyer of the parish.
All the energy you perceive as negative and
counter to your desires for your people
is born of fear.
It is fear that causes them
to array forces against you.
It is fear that fuels their gossip and complaints.
The most difficult person within the congregation
is the one who is most afraid.

"Perfect love casts out fear."
So if you would love your people,
do not be afraid of them,
for they cannot hurt you
and you are not their enemy.
See through their fears
and show them safety.

Observations
Think now of the most difficult person in your congregation. Is there a way to lessen his or her fear?

Thought 47 - The Heart

The work of the Word is done within your heart,
not within your mind.
Within your heart lies all love and peace,
and it is your heart you must give.

Your actions and words
are demanded by the parish,
"Do this and that and we will be satisfied.
Say this and that and we will be pleased."

But it is your heart they truly need.
For from your heart,
and not from your achievements,
comes the healing power of God.

Observations
How would you go about giving your heart to your parish? Don't do
it by constant activity. Don't do it by trying to accomplish more and
more. People can tell the difference between a pastor who loves them
and one who is merely busy.

Thought 48 - Subtraction

Education has daily added
more and more things
to your pastoral bag of tricks.
Practice of the Word
subtracts each day from the bag,
until at last there is nothing left.
And since your bag is empty,
you have no way to force things
and shape things
according to your will.
And only then do you live the prayer,
"Not my will but Thine be done."

Observations
A paradox once again. I empty myself in order to be filled. On which pastoral tricks in your bag are you the most dependent? How hard will it be to empty that bag?

Thought 49 - Leadership

The pastor refuses to impose her mind.

Instead she honors the minds of her people.

She treats all within the parish

as lovable and trustworthy,

even when they are not.

This makes her difficult to understand.

People wait for her to lead.

Instead she waits for them to know

the voice within their own soul

which will lead them perfectly.

Observations

Perhaps the greatest spiritual temptation facing a pastor is the pressure to provide "leadership."

People love to see buildings built and pews packed. The dynamic and forceful leader can accomplish these things and more. Everyone is pleased. Denominational leaders are pleased, parishioners are proud of their "leader," and the pastor has the world by the tail.

And hundreds of souls wither for lack of exercise.

Thought 50 - Non-Grasping

The pastor knows that the parish
does not belong to him.
He does not need to grasp it.
He has no illusions about his own importance.
He does not resist
the natural ebb and flow of things.
Therefore he has no need to hold back
and can give himself to each task
naturally, effortlessly, and completely.
And when it is time for him to leave,
he does so as easily as going to sleep
at the end of a satisfying day's work.

Observations
This place is *not* your career.
You are *not* a professional religious person.
You *are* a soul, naked before God like all other souls.
Let go.

Thought 51 - Freedom

Every person within your congregation
is an expression of God.
Each is being perfectly who they are.
Each is loved, nurtured, and protected by God.
And each is called home to God,
completing a great journey.

God loves and guides
without coercing or interfering.
That is how God's love so naturally
permeates the whole of creation.
When the pastor is centered in the Word
she is free to act as God acts,
without need or agenda.
Thus she is free.

Observations
Just for today:
There is no one who needs to act differently, behave more pleasingly
or shape up in any manner whatsoever.
How does that feel?

Thought 52 - Origins

If you were to trace all things back to their beginning,
you would find the Word.
If you were to follow all things out to their ending,
you would find the Word.

When you are confused and troubled
by events and persons in your parish,
look deeply into the origins of the problem
and you will find the Word
and you will find wisdom.

If you do not do this work,
you will make hasty judgments
and decide according to your own desires.
This will keep you in constant turmoil.
If instead you look into the origins of things
you will find light for your heart.
And as your judgments fall away
that light will shine upon the congregation.

Observations
Examine the areas of your parish that seem in the most turmoil right
now. Look more deeply into these situations, not with worry or fear,
but with a desire for light. Somewhere at the heart of the situation will
be the clarity of God.

Thought 53 - Simple

Following the Word is effortless and simple,
but your people will prefer harder,
more complicated ways
because they carry the illusion of productivity.

You will be able to tell when the balance has shifted.
There will be an increase in activity
and a decrease in thoughtfulness.
There will be an increase in effort
and a decrease in peace.
There will be an increase in exciting programs
and a decrease in wise and simple people.
There will be an increase in talking
and a decrease in listening.

Stay pure and simple
for this is the way of the Word.

Observations
This is true internally as well. How do you feel right now? Are you
trying too hard? Talking too much?

Thought 54 - Not Hidden

The Word is not an elusive fugitive.

It does not hide from the congregation

nor does it hover just out of their reach.

Wherever genuine caring is seen,

the Word is present.

Wherever pain is genuinely felt,

and faced without fear,

the power of the Word is near.

Whenever people hear each other

without judgment or agenda,

the Word is heard.

Wherever a flower opens,

or fades,

the Word is seen.

There is no need to labor

to convince people of this truth.

Simply stand quietly and point.

Observations

Try spending a day simply noticing every thing and every event that speaks of God. Physically or verbally point to it without attempting to explain, describe, or convince. Trust God and other people to connect with each other simply and easily.

Thought 55 - Health

Disappointment causes the spirit to wither.
Frustration causes the heart to contract.
Anxiety causes the body to shake.
Although the pastor knows these states,
he has released them.

His spirit is not expecting his people
to be anything other than who they are.
So he is not disappointed
and his spirit stays young and fresh.

His heart is not set on any one result.
So he is not frustrated by events,
and his heart stays strong and vital.

He lives in the truth that he belongs to God
and has nothing to gain or lose.
So he is not anxious as he waits
for things to happen
and his body is supple and stable.

Observations
The aches and pains of your body can be quite revealing of the spiritual tensions you carry. Even those symptoms that have direct physical causes are often aggravated by frustration and fear.

Thought 56 - No Words

The ancient wisdom is so hard
for a pastor to believe:
Those who know don't talk.
Those who talk don't know.
For his world is built on his words.

Try this experiment.
Don't talk for a whole day.
Don't read anything for that same day.
Don't listen to radio
or watch television.
Don't attempt to think great thoughts.
Just dull all your senses
and see if you can get a glimpse
of who you are without these things.
Here is where the Word dwells.
No wonder it seems hard to find.

Observations
Pastors who try this experiment report finding it very difficult and frightening at first. But all find it eventually leads to a quantum jump in peace and communion with God.

Thought 57 - Let Go

If you try to teach the rules of God

you will create rule breakers.

Let go of the rules and the people will keep the Word

perfectly in their hearts.

If you try to raise money,

the parish will always struggle.

Let go of fund-raising, and that which is needed

will arise effortlessly.

If you try to teach religion,

the people will become Pharisees.

Let go of religion, and people will become spiritual

in the deepest recesses of their soul.

If you try to work for justice,

you will become self-righteous.

Let go of your concepts of justice, and righteousness will

flow like a never failing stream.

Let go of your plans,

and the parish will reflect God's Love naturally.

Observations

If you currently are involved in a project which you cannot give up because of its vital importance to peace, justice, and the Kingdom of God, you may have created an idol. Amos said that righteousness will flow like a river, and one need never push a river.

Thought 58 - No Imposition

Power will not make the people holy.
You cannot impose anything.
Impose happiness
and people are miserable.
Impose great dreams,
and people feel like failures.
Impose righteousness,
and people become sinners.

Merely serve as an example.
Your tolerance and acceptance
create serenity and comfort.
Your straightforwardness
creates security and honesty.
Your light shines,
but never blinds.
It illuminates others,
and is not seen of itself.

Thought 59 - Love

The idealistic pastor
brings trouble to his parish.
He is not free from his own ideas.
The Word does not create idealism,
it creates love.

The pastor of love
uses whatever God provides to build love.
Like a tree that bends in the wind,
he accommodates to the force of natural events
and is not overwhelmed by them.
Like the sun,
he does not discriminate among people
in giving his gift.
Like a mountain,
his presence is stable and sure.
He can do all things,
because he has released all things.
He can care for all people
because he claims none.

Observations
Are there ideas or ideals that are keeping you from love?

Thought 60 - Gardening

Pastoring a church
is like tending a small garden.
If you keep pulling up the plants
to see if the roots are growing,
you will gather nothing.

If you resist and fight
every time there is trouble in the church,
you give evil its power.
Merely move aside
as would a martial arts master,
and evil will collapse of its own weight
on the floor beside you.

Observations
What would happen if you stepped aside from the conflicts in which
you are currently involved?

Thought 61 - Greatness

If your church should grow large,
your challenge is great.
For you will be tempted to think,
"I did this."
You then have something to prove,
and something to lose;
and you cannot live the Word
with something to prove and something to lose.

If you make a mistake
your reward is great.
For you can admit it
and correct it.
Your greatest friends are those
who honestly point out your mistakes.
Your greatest enemy
is your own illusion of greatness.

Your parish flourishes
when it heals and nurtures its people.
Their health becomes a beacon,
guiding others,
not to your doors,
but to their own souls.

Thought 62 - Good News

You may bring honor to your parish
and to yourself with eloquent pulpit messages.
You may win the admiration of all
within your congregation
because of your tireless work on their behalf.
But the treasure beyond all treasures will elude you.
It is at the center of all things,
beyond all achievement,
beyond success and failure,
available to winner and loser alike.

A pastor looking for wisdom
is frequently offered Ten Church Growth Principles,
when he should be offered
a way to the Word.
If the pastor is one with the Word,
he finds whatever he needs.
He is forgiven whenever he falls.
This is the Good News.

Observations
What are you working for today? Be specific. Whatever is on the
agenda for today, ask, "Why?" There may be a satisfying answer;
there may not be.

Thought 63 - Problems

Problems are no problem
to the pastor of the Word.
When she encounters a difficulty
she embraces it.
Since she is one with Love,
she does not fear the difficulty,
the negative person,
the criticism,
the obstacle.
Since she is not afraid,
she does not need to avoid the problem.
She can welcome it into her heart
while it is still small.
Since it is still small,
it resolves itself – no problem.

Observations
Take the problem that is currently perplexing you and reframe your
attitude toward it. Welcome it. Cherish it. See it with gratitude. Like
the knot in a muscle releases under the hands of a skilled massage
therapist, so will your problem release under your loving touch.

Thought 64 - Small Steps

Wherever you see kindness and love,
nourish these seeds.
Tiny hints of discord
can be noticed early by the mindful pastor
and can easily be turned to peace.
But if you are blindly pursuing
your agendas and purposes,
you ignore these tiny seeds
and reap a later harvest of great trouble.

Seeds of love can only be fed and watered;
they cannot be forced to grow.
The wise pastor waters and waits.
He does not have to teach the seed to grow;
it grows because of what it is.
He does not have to teach the people to grow;
he only has to remind them of who they are.
He is never impatient
for the only step necessary in the thousand mile journey
is the next one.

Observations
You do not have to get it all done now. You will always have things to do. Only one question is helpful. What is the next, small step? What does the next 15 minutes hold? No need to think further than that.

Thought 65 - Answers

The more the pastor tries to teach about God,
the less the people know God.
Talk about God can create the illusion
that holiness is being fostered.
But experience of the Word is quite different
than knowledge of words about God.
The pastor does not give answers;
she helps her people find their own answers
inside.

Observations
When you teach or preach, are you trying to get people to see it your way? Or are you helping them to discover their way – their own authentic way?

Thought 66 - Dreams

A congregation does not exist
to fulfill the needs of its pastor.
You are not the dreamer
of your people's dreams,
nor are they the characters
in your life's play.
They dream their own dreams,
and live their own lives,
if they are so encouraged.
Attempt to understand the dreams of each person
and give those dreams
a welcome place to grow.
Because you are not striving
for your own way,
no one wastes energy
striving with you.

Observations
Do you know the personal dreams of each person in your parish?
Could you ask them? It would make for fascinating conversation.

Thought 67 - Losses

The education of a pastor is a complex process.
What is lost is simplicity of thought.
Simple, clear, direct thinking
born of the silence within the heart
will keep your soul in God.

Church development takes much pastoral time.
What is lost is patient waiting.
Souls are really what we're growing,
and these will grow at their own pace.
Blessed is the pastor who has learned to wait
for souls to blossom.

Taking care of others will drain a pastor's strength.
What is lost is compassion for his own soul.
How can he pretend to love the Spirit,
when his own receives so little care?
Every soul within the congregation is blessed
when he keeps his own alive and well.

A pastor's life is spread so thin.
What is lost is depth.
Go deep, not thin.

Thought 68 - Play

The wise pastor approaches the serious
business of the church
with a spirit of laughter and play,
like a child at frolic with her playmates.
Because she has nothing to gain,
she has no need to compete
with herself,
with her colleagues,
or with the congregation.
The work is important,
the spirit is light.

Observations
Do you play or compete? In our culture it is sometimes hard to tell the difference. Is your work fun? If not, your people are being cheated.

Thought 69 - Opposition

If someone opposes your plans
do not think that you have an enemy.
You will have an enemy
only if you make him so in your heart.
Wait and see.
Perhaps your opponent is an angel
sent from God
to show you more subtle
and deeper aspects of the Word.

Let your so-called opponent
show his true intention.
If he is truly in opposition to you,
your waiting and patience
and lack of attack
will give you the victory
that redeems you both.

Observations
My opponent is *not* my enemy. He is a gift of God to help me refine
my spirit. What opposition are you facing right now? Wonderful!

Thought 70 - No Thinking

The Word is easy for a pastor to hear,
and simple to practice in the parish.
Yet if she tries to understand it
with her rational mind,
she will miss it.
If she tries to practice it
from her head
she will fail.

It is counter to conventional wisdom
and must be known with the heart
and with the body.
Not thinking, she will be in perfect communion
with the Spirit of God.

Observations
I would never suggest that you become irrational. But we all need more *non*-rational approaches to our work. Can you stop trying to think your way through every situation? Let the Holy Spirit guide you in the use of your intuition.

Thought 71 - Confidence

A confident pastor is not one who knows
what a congregation should do.
A confident pastor is one who knows
that he does not know.
His confidence comes from being healed
of the need to know.
Having been healed, he brings wholeness
to the congregation.
And the knowledge of what to do
emerges naturally.

Observations
When a denominational executive asks you, "Where is your church going?" please answer him or her honestly with. "I'm not at all sure, but the ride is wonderful!"

71

Thought 72 - Reverence

A sense of reverence and awe
in the Presence of God
cannot be learned,
cannot be taught.
Without awe, people turn to doctrine.
Without reverence people turn to rules.
Doctrine and rules can be taught and learned.

The pastor resists the temptation to teach.
She steps out of the way and points
to the Presence of God.
Reverence and awe are born in the people's hearts.

Observations
Do you have a room, some specific place such that you always take off
your shoes before entering it? Everyone needs such a room. Taking
off one's shoes is a classic act of reverence. It allows the body and soul
to notice the holiness of all ground.

Thought 73 - Never

The Word of God
never needs defending,
never overcomes by force,
never wins through competition,
never works according to our plan,
and never fails to accomplish Its purpose
of bringing all things in heaven and earth
into the wholeness of God's love.
Why would a pastor ever worry?

Observations
The best antidote to worry I know is gentle physical activity. Take a walk and think of nothing. Fill your mind only with the natural things you encounter on your walk: flowers, birds, and trees. God's Spirit will work best while you rest.

Thought 74 - Future

Anxiousness about the future
destroys the life of a congregation.
Out of this anxiousness the pastor and people
try to control events.
This is a tremendous waste of energy,
and drains the people of spiritual power.
Events are always changing
and nothing can be grasped.
If a pastor can free himself and his people
from the fear of death,
there is nothing they cannot achieve.

Observations
Do congregations die? Of course they do. They have birthdays and go through stages of growth. They search for meaning and struggle against fear. They eventually die. Realizing this can be a wonderfully freeing insight for a fearful congregation. "We will die. Therefore how shall we live in the meantime?"

Thought 75 - Space

If there is constant pressure to give and serve,

the congregation becomes starved for spiritual peace.

If programs have to be maintained

by pastoral pressure,

the people have no room to breathe.

The wise pastor trusts the people

and gives them all the space they need.

Observations

Trust is the issue. Do you trust that the people of your church, at the deepest level of their souls, are longing for God? Do you trust God's ability to satisfy this longing? Then back off and give them room.

Thought 76 - Dance

A healthy plant is supple and flexible,
moving and dancing in the wind.
A healthy congregation is also pliant,
delighting in the Wind of the Spirit.

When a plant becomes dry and brittle,
it snaps in the slightest wind.
If a congregation becomes rigid,
the Wind of the Spirit will be too much for it to take.

The pastor, having nothing to lose,
moves freely with the Wind,
and shows his congregation how to dance.

Observations

Since the body and spirit are so intertwined, I usually encourage clients to practice some form of physical activity that gently encourages suppleness in the body. Too many pastors exercise the same way they work - building endurance, competing, winning. These things have some limited value but a body that remains flexible usually houses a soul of the same quality.

Thought 77 - Balance

A pastor working according to the Word
restores balance in the congregation.
Where there is too much,
he reduces.
Where there is too little,
he adds.
His people are neither overly busy,
nor lazy and idle.
He resists the temptation to control them
to protect his position.
He does not need to take credit,
for he already has all he needs.
He does not need to succeed,
for he is perfectly himself already.

Observations

My community is filled with churches that have too much going on. They pride themselves in their extensive programming, but they have lost balance. People behind the scenes become fatigued.

Do you need to add or subtract? Are you as a parish doing one or two things with all your heart and soul, or are you doing a dozen things with fatigue and frustration?

Thought 78 - Evil

Evil cannot enter the pastor's heart,

for she has given up needing anything.

She does not need to help others,

so she is free to help without strings.

She does not need to protect herself,

so she can speak without evasion and deceit.

She does not need to prove herself,

so she can overcome hardness with flexibility.

She does not need to hold on to anything,

so she can bring serenity to sorrow.

The ability to see the paradox of the Word,

that gentleness is stronger than hardness,

is the greatest protection from evil and illusion.

Observations

Without paradox, evil would increase – for paradox counters the rigid thinking which is the breeding ground for conflict.

As an exercise, go through the Gospel of Matthew and copy all the sayings of Jesus that have a paradoxical, seemingly contradictory nature. Keep one or two of these sayings in the back of your mind at all times as a protection against rigidity of thought.

Thought 79 - The Blame Game

If the pastor seeks to blame
either himself or the congregation,
the blaming will never stop.

The pastor welcomes failure.
Because of it, he is able to
correct his illusions,
refine his spirit,
and model his humanity.
In this wonderful situation
there is never need for blame.

Observations
A simple breath prayer that helps me when I am tempted to slip into blaming myself or others for a situation is:
> "What is, is."
> "What is not, is not."
> "God is."

Don't analyze it. Just repeat it over and over to yourself when you find yourself in the blame game.

Thought 80 - The Church

A church wisely centered in the Word
produces great contentment for the people.
The activities of the church keep them
just busy enough to gain satisfaction,
but do not detract from their loved ones.
They enjoy their pastor
because they do not expect him to be
other than what he is.
Their spirits are nurtured gently
by quiet and solitude and room to be.
They care for one another
without needing certain responses in return.
They share food and song,
sorrow and joy,
and become more and more free from fear.
And when they die they think,
"It was good, is good and will be good."

Observations

Keep this image of the church in your mind. Let it serve as a touchstone whenever you become tempted to build another monument to pride and ego. We don't need any more monuments. We need a great many more Sanctuaries of the Holy Spirit.

Thought 81 - The Pastor

The more eloquent words are,
the more they may obscure the Word,
for the Word does not need eloquence
to accomplish its work.

The pastor is a simple person.
She gains by giving.
He leads by being.

Observations
Yours is a difficult, impossible, frustrating, and spirit-killing profession if practiced without simplicity and freedom.

Practiced with simplicity and freedom it is a noble, rewarding, delightful dance with the Spirit of God and with the souls of people. I pray for all pastors, everywhere. You are so deeply needed in our world.

Be yourself. Be gentle. Be happy.

God bless you.